My Mass

by Piera Paltro

Translated by Daughters of St. Paul
Illustrated by Anna Maria Curti

Pauline
BOOKS & MEDIA
BOSTON

Graphics: M. Luisa Benigni

Original Title: *La Mia Messa*

© Figlie di San Paolo, Rome, 1981

ISBN 0-8198-4765-8

English edition, copyright © 1998, 1992 by the Daughters of St. Paul

Printed and published in the U.S.A. by Pauline Books & Media, 50 St. Paul's Avenue, Boston, MA 02130-3491.

http://www.pauline.org

Pauline Books & Media is the publishing house of the Daughters of St. Paul, an international congregation of women religious serving the Church with the communications media.

1 2 3 4 5 6   03 02 01 00 99 98

Hi, God, it's me.
Could I talk with you
for a few minutes?
I have some important things
to tell you.
I want to tell you what I've learned
about you and your son Jesus....
I know that you yourself
taught me some of these things.
Jesus, your son,
has said that he gives us
his Holy Spirit
to teach us too.

We begin...

Every Sunday, dear God,
my mother and father
take me to Mass with them.
Father Anthony, our priest,
calls it "Eucharist,"
and even "liturgy," but it
must be the same thing.
At least that's
what I think.

I want to tell my friends,
Jason and Kara, all about the Mass.
But first, let me tell you
what I'll say.

4

A special greeting

When I'm playing ball
with my friends,
I can't think of
anything else.
Instead, sometimes
when I get to church,
many other things come to my mind.
I'm glad that Father Anthony
starts Mass by saying:

**"IN THE NAME
OF THE FATHER,
AND OF THE SON,
AND OF THE HOLY SPIRIT."**

This helps me begin
by thinking of you.
Then the priest says a few words
to welcome us.
He doesn't say: "Hi!"

He says: **"THE LORD BE WITH YOU."**

I really like that greeting.
It means that we are all there with Jesus.

Lord, have mercy!

Father, do you remember
the day I
got my new bicycle?
I was so happy that
I couldn't keep still at Mass.
My dad gave me a stern look
because Father Anthony
had just asked us to
quietly think of our sins
and ask for forgiveness.
Well, then I tried very hard
to think about
how good and forgiving Jesus is...
and not about my bike.
I know that when we come to church
to be with you, our hearts
should be open and honest.

So, while everyone was quiet,
I told Jesus that I had answered my mother back,
and fought with my sister, and even said some bad words.
I didn't talk to Jesus out loud, but I know he heard me.
After that I felt ready to celebrate.

6

Glory to God!

If we shout "Hooray!"
for athletes on TV,
why can't we shout
"Hooray for God!"?
After all, you're the only one who is
all holy, all loving and all good.

It's fun to say **"GLORY TO GOD"** with everybody.
When we tell you, all together, that you are holy and good,
it sounds like a cheer. I like it!
Sometimes when I say **"GLORY TO GOD,"** I feel like
singing and dancing up and down the aisles of our church.
I think that if Jesus were a boy again, he would
feel the same way.

Let us pray

When Father Anthony says,
in such an important way,
"LET US PRAY,"
it makes me think of Jesus
talking to you.

I can imagine how happy you were
to listen to him! So I listen
to Father Anthony.
I like what he says.
I think everyone does.

But to be honest, God,
I have to say that
I really don't understand
everything that Father Anthony
asks you. For example,
he never talks about me.
He doesn't say
that I need to study more.
He never talks about my grandfather
who's been sick for a long time.
My religion teacher is right.
She says that the prayer the priest says
is special.
It's not just my prayer,
like my morning and night prayers.
It's the prayer of everyone.
So I listen very closely—
as if Father Anthony
were saying it just for me.

9

The Word of God!

You know what, God?
I wish I could go on TV
like the sports announcers.
If I could, I would
read your Word
for everyone to hear.
I wouldn't do it
to show off. No, I'd do it
because your Word is beautiful.
It says things which
are different from
all the other words people say.
That's because your Word
is not made-up. It's the real
story of everything you did
because you love us.

We listen to your Word
at every Mass.
It teaches us to love and live
like your son Jesus.

So whoever wants to know
what they should do to love you
only needs to come to church
and listen.
I wish I could bring
everybody to church, at least once.
But if they all came, we would need
a church as big as the whole world!

11

Alleluia

I'm sure, dear Father,
that when Jesus was young like me,
he liked to sing. I bet he had a
great voice, too. Because you are
so wonderful, I want to tell you this:
I'm very proud of my father and mother,
and since you are my Father too,
I'm even more proud of you!
So when it's time to sing
"ALLELUIA, ALLELUIA," I sing with
all my heart. I sing to make up
for the people who insult you
when they get mad about something.
They use your name in the wrong way.

You know, God, I'd like to sing and play
all the musical instruments in the world.
And I'd like to sing and play
especially for you!
Anyway, you are God our Father
and you deserve praise
from everybody.
This is what **ALLELUIA** means.

Yes, Father Anthony

My grandmother calls it "the sermon."
My mother says,
"it's when the priest talks."
I know that this part of the Mass
is called the "homily." Anyhow,
I like it when Father Anthony talks to us.
It seems that he's looking right at me
all the time he's talking.
He says things which teach me
more about you, God,
and about your son Jesus.
Father Anthony is very nice.

I went to another church once,
and I couldn't understand the homily.
Do you remember, God?
I was wiggling all over the seat.
And my mother was upset with me.
I tried to keep still by counting all
those little squares on the ceiling of the church.
That was hard!
Oh, well.... Now I understand that I was
supposed to try to pay attention.
Next time, I will. But yesterday, Father Anthony
said beautiful things that were easy to understand.
Can you please help him to always talk that way, God?

I Believe

The other day on TV,
I heard a man say
that he doesn't believe in you, God.
I wish I could tell that man
that I know you and believe in you!
I really like it at Mass
when we pray all together:
"WE BELIEVE IN ONE GOD."

I feel like saying it over and over again.
I believe in you, God, my Father,
and in your son Jesus.
Really I do!

I know that in some countries
people can't say that they believe in you.
What do you think about that, God?
Do you know what I would do
if I lived in a place like that?
Even if I were afraid of what would happen,
I'd say **"I BELIEVE"** anyway.
It's great to be free to come to church
and tell you right out loud
that we believe in you
and in your love for us.

Hear us, O Lord

I like the part of the Mass
when we all pray about
things that happen in the world.
It's called the Prayer of the Faithful.
I found out that nobody can be
selfish at Mass, because we always
say **"WE,"** when we pray.
But would it be OK sometimes
if we each ask you for special
things we need too?
I think so, because
you love all of us, one by one.

Do you remember, Father,
the time I told you
that my puppy Rover was sick?
That wasn't being selfish
because I love Rover.

At Mass I like to pray for all
the sick people in the world
and for anybody who is suffering.
I think that there must be many people
who have nobody to pray for them.
So I pray for them too.
I don't know why, but sometimes,
after we pray together
"HEAR US, O LORD,"
we all feel more friendly—
like one big family.
I guess it's because we really
are brothers and sisters
and you are our Heavenly Father.

The bread and the wine

You know, Father, sometimes I wish
I had a small field where I could grow
the grapes and the wheat
for the bread and wine used at Mass.
My grandfather says it's not easy
to be a farmer. I believe him.
But I like it very much
when Father Anthony says
that the bread and the wine are
"the work of human hands."
That means that you let us help you.
Together we make the things we need.

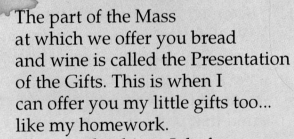

The part of the Mass
at which we offer you bread
and wine is called the Presentation
of the Gifts. This is when I
can offer you my little gifts too...
like my homework.
I can also offer you the things I do for my mom
and dad, and even the games I play.
At every Mass I offer you myself and
everything that I do. I know you like
these gifts, God.

17

Holy, holy, holy

One day, Father Anthony
explained to us the kind of glory that you have in heaven.
Wow! Dear God, you're really super special!
Millions and millions of angels and saints
all around you are always singing with joy.
Now I understand why we sing those words at Mass:
"HOLY, HOLY, HOLY."
Even though our choir in church
is not like yours in heaven, I bet it's pretty close!
But, here on earth or there in heaven,
we're all brothers and sisters, right?

Can I tell you something else?
I'd love to bring my flute to Mass one Sunday
and play it for the people who sing.
I might hit a few wrong notes...
but I know you'd understand. And maybe
even my friends could come with their instruments.
What a great orchestra that would be!
But we wouldn't play just to enjoy ourselves.
We would play to show everybody how happy we are
that you exist and are alive, God,
and that you are so great and glorious!

The Body and the Blood

The Eucharistic Prayer Father Anthony says
is a long prayer of thanksgiving
to you, God my Father.
He speaks the words of Jesus,

**"THIS IS MY BODY....
THIS IS THE CUP
OF MY BLOOD."**

At that moment of the Mass,
all that Jesus did at the Last Supper
becomes present for us.
Jesus' death on the cross
becomes present for us.
Jesus' rising to new life
becomes present for us.
Jesus is present for us!
Our simple gifts of bread and wine
have become the Body and Blood of Jesus!

This is so wonderful!
(When I finish talking to you, God,
I'm going to tell my little brother
all about it.)
If I look at the altar then, it seems to me
that Jesus is looking at me.
I can tell that all the people in church
feel the same way
because they are all so quiet.

While Jesus is there

We all proclaim
the mystery of faith.
I don't understand this mystery.
But not even my mom and dad
or even the Pope understand it,
so I don't feel bad. I know
and believe that your son Jesus
is there with us in a very,
very, special way! You have done great
things for us! I also know that Jesus is speaking
to you, Father, even more than to all of us.
I like to imagine the beautiful things that you
two are saying to one another. I know that
the Holy Spirit is with you, too. I know that
because you three are always together.
I'm sure that you also talk about me
and that makes me happy.

Dear God, I'm sure that Jesus was happy that I prayed
for the Pope, our bishop, and all those people we told you about
last Sunday. This Sunday at Mass I'm going to pray in a special way
for Jason's dad who lost his job. Will you please find him a new one?
I'm going to pray for myself, too. I need your help to be good.
I also want to ask you for good weather for my summer vacation.
I think that Jesus will say "yes," Father. Can I ask you
together with him? I trust him very much!

The great offering

Please forgive me, Father.
Yesterday I yelled at
my friend David.
And it was because of you.
David was saying that in church,
you can do the same things you do
outside.
You know, like talking and laughing
and even chewing gum.
I'm sorry, God, but I got mad. I told him
that we shouldn't do these things during
Mass
because it's the celebration of your
mystery and
the mystery of your son Jesus,
and both of you are God.

Sometimes, I seem to understand this mystery just a little more,
especially when it's very quiet and Father Anthony lifts up
to you the bread and wine which have become
the Body and Blood of Jesus. At that moment, Father Anthony
praises the great and powerful love of your son Jesus.
It is the love you share in the Holy Spirit.
Yes, **"AMEN! AMEN!"**

Our Father

Once I saw people
who were all excited about trying to read
the advertisement on a blimp flying high in the sky.
But when we pray together the

"OUR FATHER"

at Mass, we're looking up at you in a special way,
Father—
not with our eyes,
but with our hearts.
It makes me happy to know that you know and listen to
each one of us, one by one.
I really like to pray this prayer,
which my mother taught me when I was small,
with everybody at Mass.
It reminds me that all of us are one big family.
And you really are our great and good Father who loves
us very much!

25

The Sign of Peace

Do you know, Father, that something
really nice happened during Mass
last Sunday? On the way to church
my father and mother were
arguing about something.
When we got to church
I felt really bad. (You must have seen
me, right?)
My mom and dad looked so sad.
When Mass started they didn't even answer the prayers.

Then finally Father Anthony said,

"LET US OFFER EACH OTHER THE SIGN OF PEACE."

But my mom and dad wouldn't look at each other.
So I got brave and turned toward each of them
and looked them right in the eyes until they smiled at me.
Then they looked at each other too, the way they usually do.
Dear God, I wish that at least on Sundays
everybody in the world would feel like smiling at one another—
because at Mass Jesus tells us to love one another.

Jesus and I

Next in the Mass, comes the great moment of Holy Communion.
I know, my Father, that you are with me
when I go to receive your son Jesus who is coming to me.
I know that this is a very important moment.
I've made my First Communion already,
so I understand what's going on.
I know that Jesus is my older Brother,
and that he never stops loving me.
We always become closer friends.

After Holy Communion Jesus is with me
in a very special way.
He's even nearer to me
than my mother and father.
In Holy Communion Jesus
changes me and gives me
all the help I need to be loving
and good to others—
at home, at school and even when
I'm out playing.
This is why,
when I go up to receive Communion
and Father Anthony says
"THE BODY OF CHRIST," I answer:

"AMEN" with all my heart.

Thanks be to God!

Father, sometimes when it's really
nice outside, I can't wait to get
out into the sunshine again
after Mass. Do you remember the Sunday
that we were supposed to go on a picnic?
I almost ran out of church that time!
But I never leave without telling you **THANK YOU**
with all my heart.
Father Anthony does the same thing
when he prays the last prayer at Mass.
We should thank you because you are good
and you've welcomed us into your house.
Before I leave your house, God,
I make sure that I give you a beautiful smile.

Jesus is happy, too,
isn't he, Father?
I'm sure he's happy
because we came to Mass
to listen to him and
to let him come into our hearts
in Holy Communion.

Go in peace

And I also understand
that when Father Anthony says:

"GO IN PEACE,"

it doesn't only mean
that we should go home or
to some other place.
No. It means that we should
go back to doing everything
we usually do, bringing to
others a little of that Mass.
Once I didn't understand this, but now I do.
You send us home from Mass asking us
to be happy, to be generous, to be honest
and good and gentle just like Jesus.

As soon as we came out of church last Sunday,
my father said "hello" to a man who wasn't nice to him at work.
Boy, did that man looked surprised!
I was proud of my dad.
He understands that you want Sunday to be a day of peace and joy
for all people.
That's what I want too!

Well, dear God,
now you know what I understand
about the Mass,
about you and
about your son Jesus.
I've told you everything I know.
I send you a big kiss
and I thank you.
Good-bye!

BOOKS & MEDIA

The Daughters of St. Paul operate book and media centers at the following addresses. Visit, call or write the one nearest you today, or find us on the World Wide Web, www.pauline.org.

CALIFORNIA
3908 Sepulveda Blvd., Culver City, CA 90230;
  310-397-8676
5945 Balboa Ave., San Diego, CA 92111;
  619-565-9181
46 Geary Street, San Francisco, CA 94108;
  415-781-5180

FLORIDA
145 S.W. 107th Ave., Miami, FL 33174;
  305-559-6715

HAWAII
1143 Bishop Street, Honolulu, HI 96813;
  808-521-2731

ILLINOIS
172 North Michigan Ave., Chicago, IL 60601;
  312-346-4228

LOUISIANA
4403 Veterans Memorial Blvd., Metairie, LA
  70006; 504-887-7631

MASSACHUSETTS
Rte. 1, 885 Providence Hwy., Dedham, MA
  02026; 781-326-5385

MISSOURI
9804 Watson Rd., St. Louis, MO 63126;
  314-965-3512

NEW JERSEY
561 U.S. Route 1, Wick Plaza, Edison, NJ
  08817; 732-572-1200

NEW YORK
150 East 52nd Street, New York, NY 10022;
  212-754-1110
78 Fort Place, Staten Island, NY 10301;
  718-447-5071

OHIO
2105 Ontario Street (at Prospect Ave.),
  Cleveland, OH 44115; 610-621-9427

PENNSYLVANIA
9171-A Roosevelt Blvd., Philadelphia, PA
19114; 215-676-9494

SOUTH CAROLINA
243 King Street, Charleston, SC 29401;
  803-577-0175

TENNESSEE
4811 Poplar Ave., Memphis, TN 38117;
  901-761-2987

TEXAS
114 Main Plaza, San Antonio, TX 78205;
  210-224-8101

VIRGINIA
1025 King Street, Alexandria, VA 22314;
  703-549-3806

CANADA
3022 Dufferin Street, Toronto, Ontario, Canada
  M6B 3T5; 416-781-9131
1155 Yonge Street, Toronto, Ontario, Canada
  M4T 1W2; 416-934-3440

Libros en español!